Exam A

QUESTION 1

What is black ice?

A. Ice that turns black in extreme temperatures.
B. Ice that is more slippery than white ice.
C. A thin layer of ice that is clear enough that you can see the road underneath it. It makes the road look wet.
D. A thick layer of ice that is hard to see on a black top road.
E. None of the above

Section: General Knowledge

QUESTION 2

Stopping is not always the safest thing to do in an emergency.

A. True
B. False

Section: General Knowledge

QUESTION 3

Common medicines for colds can make you sleepy.

A. True
B. False

Section: General Knowledge

QUESTION 4

How frequently must you stop while on the road to check your cargo?

A. Within 25 miles after beginning a trip, after every break, and every 3 hrs, 150 miles.
B. Within 50 miles of the start of the trip.
C. Within 25 miles after beginning a trip, after every break, and every 2 hrs, 100 miles.
D. Within 30 miles of the start of the trip and after every break only thereafter.

Section: General Knowledge

QUESTION 5

Name two circumstances where legal maximum weights may not be safe to haul?

A. In large cities and over bridges.
B. During bad weather or in mountains.
C. Through tunnels and over bridges.
D. At night or during rush hour traffic.

Section: General Knowledge

QUESTION 6

Name the two basic reasons for covering cargo on an open bed?

A. To protect people from spilled cargo, and to protect the environment from spilled cargo.
B. To protect the environment from spilled cargo, and to protect the cargo from weather.
C. To protect people from spilled cargo, and to protect the cargo from weather.
D. To keep cargo secure from possible thieves and to keep cargo a secret.

Section: General Knowledge

QUESTION 7

What things should you check during a trip?

A. Manifest and shipping papers.
B. Check for load stability by slightly swerving from left to right within your lane.
C. This is how can you test the trailer emergency brakes
D. Map, directions, and weather report.
E. Watch gauges, mirrors, use your senses to check for difficulties, look, listen, smell.

Section: General Knowledge

QUESTION 8

What is the least possible tread depth for front tires?

A. 1/32
B. 2/32
C. 4/32
D. 6/32

Section: General Knowledge

QUESTION 9

When backing, why is it significant to use a helper?

A. It is easier to have the helper back the truck for you.
B. It is required by federal law.
C. It is good to have someone else around to blame if you hit something.
D. Helpers have nothing better to do than help you back up your truck.
E. Because there are blind spots you can't see.

Section: General Knowledge

QUESTION 10

What is the most significant hand sign that you and the helper should agree on?

A. Pull forward.
B. Keep Backing.
C. Stop!
D. Straighten out.

Section: General Knowledge

QUESTION 11

What three things add up to total stopping distance?

A. Perception Distance + Reaction Distance+ Braking Distance.
B. Resistance Distance + Perception Distance + Braking Distance.
C. Visual Distance+ Braking Distance + Resistance Distance.
D. Braking Distance + Perception Distance + Lag Time.
E. None of the above

Section: General Knowledge

QUESTION 12

Where your reflectors should be placed when stopped on a divided highway?

A. 20 feet, 150 feet, and 300 feet toward the approaching traffic.
B. 10 feet, 100 feet, and 200 feet toward the approaching traffic.
C. 15 feet, 75 feet, and 150 feet toward the approaching traffic.
D. 30 feet, 100 feet, and 150 feet toward the approaching traffic.

Section: General Knowledge

QUESTION 13

What is the least possible tread depth for tires other than the front tires?

A. 1/32
B. 2/32
C. 3/32
D. 4/32
E. 5/32

Section: General Knowledge

QUESTION 14

What are two main things to look for ahead while driving?

A. Road signs and detours.
B. Fire and Flooding.
C. Bridges and Tunnels.
D. Truck Stops and Police.
E. Traffic and road situations.

Section: General Knowledge

QUESTION 15

If you go twice as fast, will your stopping distance increase by two or four times?

A. Two
B. Four
C. None of the above

Section: General Knowledge

QUESTION 16

Vacant trucks have the best braking.

A. True
B. False

Section: General Knowledge

QUESTION 17

Name some suspension system faults.

A. Broken leaves in leaf spring.
B. Cracked or broken spring hangers.
C. Leaking shock absorbers.
D. All of the above.

Section: General Knowledge

QUESTION 18

What three types of backup equipment must you have?

A. Fire extinguisher, Spare electrical fuses , warning devices for parked vehicles
B. Warning devices for parked vehicles, first aid kit, flares.
C. First aid kit, fire extinguisher, flares.
D. Flares, fire extinguisher, spare electrical fuses.
E. None of the above

Section: General Knowledge

QUESTION 19

How do you test hydraulic brakes for leaks?

A. Pump the brake pedal five times, apply firm pressure for 3 seconds, the pedal should not move.
B. Hold the brake down for 5 seconds and listen for leaks.
C. Pump the brake pedal three times, apply firm pressure for 5 seconds, the pedal should not move.
D. Move slowly forward and step on the brake hard.
E. Any of the above.

Section: General Knowledge

QUESTION 20

What are the two special situations where you should downshift?

A. Before entering a curve and before going up a hill.
B. Before starting down a hiil and before entering a curve.
C. Before starting down a hill and before going up a hill.
D. If there is an accident or for sudden heavy rain.

Section: General Knowledge

QUESTION 21

What are the two ways to know when to shift?

A. Every 3 to 5 seconds or engine speed.
B. Engine speed and road speed.
C. Road speed and wind speed.
D. Engine speed and the shift indicator light.

Section: General Knowledge

QUESTION 22

You should use low beams whenever you can.

A. True
B. False

Section: General Knowledge

QUESTION 23

You can safely remove the radiator cap as long as the engine isn't overheated.

A. True
B. False

Section: General Knowledge

QUESTION 24

If a tire blows out, you should put the brakes on hard to stop fast.

A. True
B. False

Section: General Knowledge

QUESTION 25

Name two causes of tire fires?

A. Under-inflated tires and poor retreads.
B. Under-inflated tires and duals that touch.
C. Hot brakes and under-inflated tires.
D. Duals that touch and road debris.

Section: General Knowledge

QUESTION 26

When using your fire extinguisher, should you get as close as possible to the fire?

A. True

B. False

Section: General Knowledge

QUESTION 27

Coffee and a little fresh air will help a drinker sober up?

A. True

B. False

Section: General Knowledge

QUESTION 28

What is the least possible number of tied owns for any flatbed load?

A. One

B. Two

C. Four

D. Six

Section: General Knowledge

QUESTION 29

Name some things you should check on the front of your vehicle during the walk-around inspection?

A. oil, transmission, air compressor, radiator

B. Low beams, high beams, four way flashers, turn signs

C. windshield, wipers, mirrors, hood latches

D. tires, steering parts, suspension parts, headlights

E. None of the above

Section: General Knowledge

QUESTION 30

Why are placards used?

A. To avoid terrorism.
B. So hazmat is not mixed with food.
C. It is the law.
D. Communicate the threat.

Section: General Knowledge

QUESTION 31

What should you do if you do become sleepy while driving?

A. Turn up the radio.
B. Drink caffeinated beverages.
C. Roll down the windows.
D. Stop to sleep.

Section: General Knowledge

QUESTION 32

When should you down shift automatic transmissions?
A. Half way down a hill.
B. At the bottom of a hill.
C. Never.
D. Before going down a hill.
E. None of the above

Section: General Knowledge

QUESTION 33

What is your most significant way to see the sides and rear?

A. Rear view cameras.
B. Your mirrors.
C. Roll the window down.
D. A Helper.
E. All of the above.

Section: General Knowledge

QUESTION 34

What does, communicating, in safe driving mean?

A. Using a c.b. radio to let others know your intentions.
B. Letting others know you are there by using turn signs, four way flashers and horn.
C. Using hand signs
D. All of the above.
E. None of the above.

Section: General Knowledge

QUESTION 35

You should decrease your following distance if somebody is following you too closely.

A. True
B. False

Section: General Knowledge

QUESTION 36

If you swing wide to the left before turning right, another driver may try to pass you on the right.

A. True
B. False

Section: General Knowledge

QUESTION 37

What should you do before you drive if you are drowsy?

A. Take a cold shower
B. Get Sleep
C. Drink coffee
D. Do a little Exercise

Section: General Knowledge

QUESTION 38

What effects can wet brakes cause?
A. Can cause brakes to apply unevenly.
B. Can cause lack of braking power.
C. Can cause pulling to one side or the other.
D. All of the above.
E. None of the above.

Section: General Knowledge

QUESTION 39

How can you evade the effects that wet brakes can cause?

A. Slow down.
B. Gently put on the brakes. This presses linings against brake drums or discs and keeps mud, silt, sand, and water from getting in.
C. Place transmission in a low gear.
D. Increase engine rpm and cross the water while keeping light pressure on the brakes.
E. When out of the water, maintain light pressure on the brakes for a short distance to heat them up and dry them out.
F. All of the above

Section: General Knowledge

QUESTION 40

What reasons determine your selection of a safe speed when going down a long, steep downgrade?

A. Length of the grade and steepness of the grade only.
B. Total weight of the vehicle and cargo.
C. Total weight of the vehicle and cargo, length of the grade, steepness of the grade, road situations, weather.
D. Total weight of the vehicle, steepness of the grade, weather.

Section: General Knowledge

QUESTION 41

Why should you be in the correct gear before starting down a hill?

A. You will not be able to shift into a lower gear once you are going down the hill.
B. Because you will need to be in the same gear at the bottom of the hill.
C. It is the law in most states.
D. There is no need to do this.
E. Because the clutch is made to be used on even surfaces.

Section: General Knowledge

QUESTION 42

What is a hazard?

A. A hazard is more than an emergency.
B. A hazard is a material that you haul that requires placards.
C. A hazard is any road condition or other road user that is a possible danger.
D. A hazard is a truck with no placards that has dangerous materials.

Section: General Knowledge

QUESTION 43

What is a benefit of going right instead of left around a hindrance?

A. If the shoulder is paved, going right may be best. No one is ever on the shoulder; someone could be passing you on the left.
B. There is no benefit.
C. It is much easier to turn a truck to the right than it is to the left. It is good to make a habit out of going the same way every time.
D. If you are blocked on both sides, a move to the right, At least you won't force anyone into an opposing traffic lane and a possible head on collision.

Section: General Knowledge

QUESTION 44

What can you do at an accident scene to avoid another accident?

A. Put on your flashers.
B. Set out reflective triangles to warn other traffic.
C. If your vehicle is involved in the accident; try to get it to the side of the road.
D. If you are stopping to help, park away from the accident.
E. All of the above.

Section: General Knowledge

QUESTION 45

For what three things related to cargo are drivers responsible?

A. Inspecting your cargo, recognizing overloads, correctly secured cargo.
B. Inspecting your cargo, hauling cargo and securing the cargo.
C. Weighing the cargo, securing the cargo, delivering the cargo.
D. None of the above.

Section: General Knowledge

QUESTION 46

What is a dangerous materials placard?

A. Signs put on the outside of a vehicle which identify the hazard class of the cargo.
B. Signs put on the back of a vehicle which identifies the hazard class of the cargo.
C. Signs put on the outside of a vehicle which identify the hazard class and weight of the cargo.
D. Signs put on the inside of a vehicle which identify the hazard class of the cargo.

Section: General Knowledge

QUESTION 47

Which of the following statements is false?

A. Gross Combination Weight (GCW). The total weight of a powered unit plus trailers.
B. Gross Combination Weight (GCW). The total weight of a powered unit plus trailers plus the cargo.
C. Gross Combination Weight Rating (GCWR). The maximum GCW specified by the manufacturer for a specific combination of vehicles plus its load.
D. They are all true.

Section: General Knowledge

QUESTION 48

What must you check before transporting a sealed load?

A. The placard numbers match the seal numbers.
B. That the seal is authentic.
C. That the seal is secure.
D. The load is correctly secured.

Section: General Knowledge

QUESTION 49

How do you find out how many seconds of following distance space you have?

A. Wait until the vehicle ahead passes a clear landmark, then count off the seconds until you reach the same spot.
B. Wait until the vehicle ahead passes a clear landmark, then count off the seconds until you reach the same spot. Then multiply times 2.
C. Divide your speed by four and add one second for every 10 feet of trailer in the day and 2 seconds at night.
D. Divide your speed by four and add one second for every 10 feet of trailer.
E. None of the above.

Section: General Knowledge

QUESTION 50

Why make emergency plans when you see a hazard?

A. You will have more time to act if you see hazards before they become emergencies.
B. You will have less time to act if you see hazards before they become emergencies.
C. So you will have a plan to communicate the threat.
D. Because all hazards turn into emergencies.

Section: General Knowledge

QUESTION 51

What is a pull-up?

A. A manuver performed by a tow truck to pick up an overturned truck.
B. An exercise that must be performed at a d.o.t. physical exam in order to get a C.D.L.
C. When pulling off the shoulder you pull up untill the trailer is straight.
D. Pulling forward while backing a trailer to reposition it.

Section: General Knowledge

QUESTION 52

Brake hard enough to feel a slowdown, when your speed has been moderated to 5 mph below your safe speed, release the brakes.

A. When your speed has increased to your safe speed, repeat these steps.
B. This is the procedure for a blown tire.
C. This is the procedure for driving on slippery roads.
D. This is the procedure for coming down long steep grades.
E. All of the above.

Section: General Knowledge

QUESTION 53

What is hydroplaning?

A. A term used for fast planning an alternate route due to heavy rain.
B. When tires lose their contact with the road and have little or no traction due to water on the road.
C. The amount of traction a truck has due to the weight of the vehicle on slippery surfaces.
D. A water spill on the road that came from a water truck.

Section: General Knowledge

QUESTION 54

What is an escape ramp?

A. A ramp commonly found on freeways in California used to get around main accidents.
B. Another term for an off ramp.
C. A ramp leading to a long bed of loose soft material to slow a runaway vehicle, sometimes in combination with an upgrade.
D. None of the above

Section: General Knowledge

QUESTION 55

What should wheel bearing seals be checked for?
A. Color changes
B. Smoke
C. Leaks
D. Gasoline
E. All of the above.

Section: General Knowledge

QUESTION 56

Which of the following is not a common cause of vehicle fires?

A. Electrical short circuits due to loose connections.

B. Imcorrect use of flares.
C. Loose air lines.
D. Imcorrectly sealed flammable cargo.
E. Spilled fuel after an accident.

Section: General Knowledge

QUESTION 57

You have just started your first job with an over the road trucking company. A couple of months go by and you realize that you are driving in the same weather, on the same roads, and hauling the same stuff for half of what other drivers are making! What should you do?

A. Abandon the truck and take the bus home
B. Just drive for half the money
C. Accept the fact you will be living in a truck the rest of your life and broke
D. Get the Ebook at Richtruckdriver.com and start planning to get a real truck driver job!

Section: General Knowledge

QUESTION 58

What kind of air do air brakes use?

A. Decompressed air
B. Warm air
C. Compressed air
D. Heated air

Section: Air Brakes

QUESTION 59

Which of the following is a valve used at the back of a trailer that allows the closing of the air lines when another trailer is not being towed?

A. Drain valve
B. Cut-out cocks
C. Dummy coupler
D. Tractor protection valve

Section: Combination Vehicles

QUESTION 60

Which of the following devices should you use to avoid water and dirt from getting into the coupler and air lines when they are not in use?

A. Dead end or dummy couplers
B. Shut-off valves
C. Relay valves
D. Tractor protection valve

Section: Combination Vehicles

QUESTION 61

How are the airlines color coded to keep them from getting mixed up?

A. Emergency line is BLUE. Service line is RED.

B. Emergency line is RED. Service line is WHITE.

C. Emergency line is GREEN. Service line is BLUE.

D. Emergency line is RED. Service line is BLUE.

Section: Combination Vehicles

QUESTION 62

You could experience steering difficulties because of friction amid the tractor and trailer if you do not lubricate which of the following?

A. Relay valves
B. Glad hands
C. Fifth wheel plate
D. Dead end couplers

Section: Combination Vehicles

QUESTION 63

If you are lowering the landing gear of a loaded trailer, you should

A. Lift the trailer off of the fifth wheel
B. Lower the landing gear until it makes firm contact with the ground
C. Turn the crank in low gear a few extra turns after firm contact with the ground
D. Turn the crank in high gear a few extra turns after firm contact with the ground

Section: Combination Vehicles

QUESTION 64

Which shut-off valves should be open and which closed?

A. All shut-off valves should be closed
B. All shut-off valves should be open
C. The front trailers shut-off valves open and the rear closed
D. The rear trailers shut-off valves open and the front closed

Section: Combination Vehicles

QUESTION 65

What might happen if the trailer is too high when you try to couple?

A. It may not couple correctly
B. The king pin may fall off
C. The trailer may tip and flip over
D. All of the above

Section: Combination Vehicles

QUESTION 66

What is the emergency air line for?

A. It supplies air to the tractor air tanks and controls the service brakes on combination vehicles
B. It supplies air to the trailer air tanks and controls the service brakes on combination vehicles
C. It supplies air to the trailer air tanks and controls the emergency brakes on combination vehicles
D. It supplies air to the tractor air tanks and controls the emergency brakes on combination vehicles
E. None of the above

Section: Combination Vehicles

QUESTION 67

What two things are significant to avoid rollover?

A. Evenly loaded trailer and correctly inflated tires
B. Keeping the cargo as close to the ground as possible and drive slowly around turns
C. The weight and length of the vehicle
D. Keeping the cargo center of gravity as high as possible and drive slowly around turns

Section: Combination Vehicles

QUESTION 68

What is off tracking?

A. Off tracking is when the front wheels follow a different path than the front wheels

B. Off tracking is when the rear wheels go into a skid and the front wheels continue in a straight line

C. Off tracking is when the front wheels go one direction and the trailer wheels go in the other direction

D. Off tracking is when the rear wheels follow a different path than the front wheels

E. None of the above

Section: Combination Vehicles

QUESTION 69

After coupling, how much space should be amid the upper and lower fifth wheel?

A. 1/32 inch

B. 1/16 inch

C. 1/8 inch

D. 1/4

E. None of the above

Section: Combination Vehicles

QUESTION 70

When you turn unexpectedly while pulling double trailers which trailer is most possible to turn over?

A. The front trailer

B. The rear trailer

C. Both trailers

D. Neither trailer is more possible to turn over

E. None of the above

Section: Combination Vehicles

QUESTION 71

To drive you need to raise the landing gear only until it just lifts off the pavement.

A. True
B. False

Section: Combination Vehicles

QUESTION 72

Why should you not use the trailer hand brake to straighten out a jackknifing trailer?

A. The trailer wheels caused the skid in the first place. Once the trailer wheels grip the road again, the trailer will start to follow the tractor and straighten out
B. The tractor wheels caused the skid in the first place. Once the trailer wheels grip the road again, the trailer will start to follow the tractor and straighten out
C. The tractor wheels caused the skid in the first place. Once the trailer wheels grip the road again, the trailer will start to push the tractor and straighten out
D. This is the only time that you should use the trailer brake
E. None of the above

Section: Combination Vehicles

QUESTION 73

You should look into the back of the fifth wheel to see if it is locked onto the kingpin

A. True
B. False

Section: Combination Vehicles

QUESTION 74

Which of the following best describes what the trailer air supply control does?

A. You pull it out to supply the trailer with air, and push it in to shut the air off and put on the trailer emergency brakes
B. You push it in to supply the tractor with air, and pull it out to supply the trailer with air
C. You push it in to supply the trailer with air, and pull it out to shut the air off and put on the trailer emergency brakes
D. You push it in to supply the trailer with air, and pull it out to supply the tractor with air

Section: Combination Vehicles

QUESTION 75

Where are shut-off valves?

A. At the front of each trailer
B. At the back of each trailer
C. At the front and back of each trailer
D. On converter dollies

Section: Combination Vehicles

QUESTION 76

Why should you not use the trailer hand valve while driving?.

A. It should not be used it in driving because the trailer brakes will not be applied evenly
B. It is ok to use it while driving on dry roads
C. It should not be used it in driving because it releases too much air from the system
D. It should not be used it in driving because of the danger of making the trailer skid

Section: Combination Vehicles

QUESTION 77

Describe what the service line is for.

A. It carries air which is controlled by the foot brake or the trailer hand brake
B. It carries air which is controlled by the foot brake
C. It carries air which is controlled by the trailer hand brake
D. All of the above

Section: Combination Vehicles

QUESTION 78

Why should you use chocks when parking a trailer without spring brakes?

A. If the air supply in the service air tank has leaked away there will be no emergency brakes enabling the trailer wheels to turn freely
B. If the air supply in the trailer air tank has leaked away there will be no emergency brakes enabling the trailer wheels to turn freely
C. If the air supply in the trailer air tank has leaked away there will be no emergency brakes enabling the tractor wheels to turn freely
D. If the air supply in the trailer air tank has leaked away there will be no service brakes enabling the trailer wheels to turn freely

Section: Combination Vehicles

QUESTION 79

Go to the rear of the rig. Open the emergency line shut-off valve at the rear of the last trailer. You should hear air escaping, showing the entire system is charged. Close the emergency line valve. Open the service line valve to check that service pressure goes through all the trailers (this test assumes that the trailer handbrake or the service brake pedal is on), then close the valve. If you do NOT hear air escaping from both lines, check that the shut-off valves on the trailer(s) and dolly(s) are in the OPEN position.

A. This is no way to test anything
B. This is how can you test the tractor protection valve
C. This is how can you test the trailer emergency brakes
D. This is how can you test that air flows to all trailers
E. This is how can you test the trailer service brakes

Section: Combination Vehicles

QUESTION 80
Charge the trailer air brake system and check that the trailer rolls freely. Then stop and pull out the trailer air supply control valve. Pull gently on the trailer with the tractor to check that the trailer emergency brakes are on.

A. This is no way to test anything
B. This is how can you test the tractor protection valve
C. This is how can you test the trailer emergency brakes
D. This is how can you test that air flows to all trailers
E. This is how can you test the trailer service brakes

Section: Combination Vehicles

QUESTION 81

Check for standard air pressure, release the parking brakes, move the vehicle forward slowly, and apply trailer with the hand control trolley valve, if so equipped

A. This is no way to test anything
B. This is how can you test the tractor protection valve
C. This is how can you test the trailer emergency brakes
D. This is how can you test that air flows to all trailers
E. This is how can you test the trailer service brakes

Section: Combination Vehicles

QUESTION 82

Charge the trailer air brake system and push the air supply knob in. Shut the engine off. Step on and off the brake pedal numerous times to moderate the air pressure in the tanks. The trailer air supply control should pop out when the air pressure falls into the pressure range specified by the manufacturer.

A. This is no way to test anything
B. This is how can you test the tractor protection valve
C. This is how can you test the trailer emergency brakes
D. This is how can you test that air flows to all trailers
E. This is how can you test the trailer service brakes

Section: Combination Vehicles

QUESTION 83

You have just started your first job with an over the road trucking company. A couple of months go by and you realize that you are driving in the same weather, on the same roads, and hauling the same stuff for half of what other drivers are making! What should you do?

A. Abandon the truck and take the bus home
B. Just drive for half the money
C. Accept the fact you will be living in a truck the rest of your life and broke
D. Get the Ebook at Richtruckdriver.com and start planning to get a real truck driver job

Section: Combination Vehicles

QUESTION 84

What is rearward amplification?

A. Weight transfer to the rear axles when going up a hill in a double/triple
B. 'Crack-the-whip' effect when making quick lane changes
C. The increased weight on the rear axles of a double or triple trailer
D. Sudden, dangerous weight shift from the front to the rear trailer

Section: Doubles Triples

QUESTION 85

In a set of triples, where should the heaviest trailer be?

A. Second trailer position
B. Third trailer position
C. Either second or third trailer position
D. First trailer position (behind the tractor)

Section: Doubles Triples

QUESTION 86

Why should you never disconnect the pintle hook with the dolly still under the rear trailer?

A. The dolly tow bar may fly up, possibly causing injury
B. The kingpin may become damaged
C. The pintle lock mechanism may become damaged
D. The emergency brake will activate

Section: Doubles Triples

QUESTION 87

When connecting the converter dolly to the front trailer, what do you do first?

A. Secure converter gear support in the upright position
B. Release dolly brakes
C. Back first semitrailer in front of dolly tongue
D. Lock pintle hook

Section: Doubles Triples

QUESTION 88

If a second trailer does not have spring brakes, how should you set the brakes when you are coupling?

A. Connect the service air line to the trailer and use the Johnson bar to work the trailer brakes.
B. Drive the tractor close to the trailer, connect the emergency line to charge the trailer air tank and disconnect the emergency line
C. Manually adjust the slack adjusters to move the brake shoes in contact with the trailer brake drums
D. Connect the service air line to the trailer and press down on the brake pedal while you connect the trailer

Section: Doubles Triples

QUESTION 89

Pushing in the trailer air supply knob will do what?

A. Supply air to the service air line
B. Supply air to the emergency air line
C. Shut off air to the trailer air tank
D. Put on the emergency brakes

Section: Doubles Triples

QUESTION 90

How should you check that you have sufficient emergency airflow to all trailers in a set of doubles or triples?

A. Use the trailer hand brake to supply air. Go to the rear of the last trailer, open the service line valve and listen for air escaping.
B. Move the trailers and apply the emergency brakes.
C. Push in the red trailer air supply knob, open the emergency line shut-off valve at the rear of the last trailer and listen for air escaping.
D. Fully charge the air system, activate the emergency brakes and look for a 15 psi air pressure reduction

Section: Doubles Triples

QUESTION 91

What is the main purpose of a trailer shut-off valve?

A. It works the trailer brakes
B. To be used only for emergency stopping
C. A coupling device that connects the air lines amid converter dollies and trailers
D. To close the air lines of the last trailer to avoid air from leaking out

Section: Doubles Triples

QUESTION 92

What is the precise position of the shut-off valves for the last trailer of a doubles or triples set?

A. Fully closed
B. Fully open
C. Partially open
D. Emergency shut-off valve open; service shut-off valve closed

Section: Doubles Triples

QUESTION 93

What is the precise position of the shut-off valves for the first trailer of a doubles or triples set?
A. Fully closed
B. Fully open
C. Partially closed
D. Emergency shut-off valve closed; service shut-off valve open

Section: Doubles Triples

QUESTION 94

What is the accurate position of the converter dolly air drain valve during the pre-trip inspection?

A. Fully closed
B. Fully open
C. Partially closed
D. It does not matter

Section: Doubles Triples

QUESTION 95

Which of the following driving practice is suggested for doubles/triples?

A. Load heaviest semi-trailer in the rear position
B. No exceptional driving practices are suggested
C. Allow more following distance
D. Both A and C

Section: Doubles Triples

QUESTION 96

What is the correct amount of space amid the upper and lower parts of the fifth wheel on the dolly when coupled to a trailer?

A. 1/2 inch
B. 4/32 of an inch

C. Less than one inch
D. No space

Section: Doubles Triples

QUESTION 97

What should be examined on the landing gear for doubles/triples?

A. Fully raised with no missing parts
B. Crank handle in place and secured
C. If power operated, no air or hydraulic leaks
D. All the above

Section: Doubles Triples

QUESTION 98

Where will you find shut off valves on doubles and triples?

A. Emergency air lines
B. Service air lines
C. Trailer brake system only
D. [*]Both service and emergency air lines

Section: Doubles Triples

QUESTION 99

If your tractor protection valve malfunctions, what could happen?

A. The emergency brakes can come on
B. A leak in the air hose could drain the air
C. Air can drain from your trailer brakes
D. All of the above

Section: Doubles Triples

QUESTION 100

What is the precise procedure to test the trailer service brakes?

A. Lightly test brakes at low speed
B. Use trolley valve to apply brakes and check to see if you feel the trailer brakes come on
C. Repeatedly depress the brake pedal
D. Pull out the trailer air supply control

Section: Doubles Triples

QUESTION 101

Which trailer of a triple trailer is most likely to roll over?

A. The front trailer
B. The middle trailer
C. The rear trailer
D. All the trailers have the same chance of rolling over

Section: Doubles Triples

QUESTION 102

What is the correct trailer height when you connect the converter dolly to the rear trailer?

A. Six inches of space amid the fifth wheel and the trailer
B. Trailer is slightly lower than the center of the fifth wheel
C. The fifth wheel and the trailer are at the same height
D. The trailer is high enough so that it doesn't raise when the tractor is backed under it.

Section: Doubles Triples

QUESTION 103

Which of the following procedures should you do when connecting the converter dolly to the rear trailer?

A. Make sure trailer brakes are locked
B. Open shut-off valves at rear of last trailer
C. Insure that the trailer is slightly lower than the center of the fifth wheel
D. A and C

Section: Doubles Triples

QUESTION 104

During a pre-trip inspection of your bus, you should
A. Insure that your front tires have been recapped or regrouped
B. Insure that the emergency roof hatches are fully closed
C. Close any open access panels (baggage, engine etc.)
D. All of the above

Section: Passenger Transport

QUESTION 105

Which of the following dangerous materials is FORBIDDEN to be transported on a bus?
A. Small-arms ammunition (labeled ORM-D)
B. Emergency hospital supplies
C. Tear gas
D. All of the above

Section: Passenger Transport

QUESTION 106

Which of the following dangerous materials is ALLOWED to be transported on a bus?

A. Car batteries
B. Small-arms ammunition
C. Liquid pesticides
D. All of the above

Section: Passenger Transport

QUESTION 107

The two-inch line on the floor behind the driver's seat is identified as

A. Stand zone
B. Driver area line
C. Baggage line
D. Standee line

Section: Passenger Transport

QUESTION 108

If you have a drunk or disruptive passenger, you should

A. Immediately stop the bus and discharge them
B. Make them sit in the front of the bus, behind the driver
C. Drop the person off at the next scheduled stop or a nearby safe well-lit area
D. None of the above

Section: Passenger Transport

QUESTION 109

When dealing with a railroad crossing, you should

A. Stop 100 feet before the crossing
B. Open your forward door to look and listen for approaching train
C. Downshift while crossing the tracks
D. None of the above
E.

Section: Passenger Transport

QUESTION 110

When approaching a drawbridge with no traffic light or attendant, you should
A. Exit your vehicle to insure that the drawbridge is closed
B. Slow down and make sure it's safe
C. Stop at least 50 feet before the draw of the bridge
D. All of the above

Section: Passenger Transport

QUESTION 111

Which of the following statements is FALSE regarding brake and accelerator interlock systems?

A. The interlock applies the brakes when the rear door is open
B. The interlock holds the throttle in idle position when the rear door is open
C. You can use the interlock in place of the parking brake
D. The interlock releases when you close the rear door

Section: Passenger Transport

QUESTION 112

Which of the following practices is suggested when you have passengers on your bus?

A. Refueling in a closed building with passengers on board during cold or inclement weather
B. Requesting the passengers to leave the bus during refueling
C. Towing or pushing the bus with passengers on board
D. Having conversations with your passengers to make the ride more enjoyable

Section: Passenger Transport

QUESTION 113

If you are driving a bus around a banked curve, you should

A. Drive at the posted speed
B. Drive at the same speed as other traffic
C. Slow down if your bus leans toward the outside of the curve
D. Maintain your speed throughout the curve

Section: Passenger Transport

QUESTION 114

When should you check your vehicle?

A. Before your shift
B. After your shift
C. Before and after your shift
D. Every 500 miles

Section: Passenger Transport

QUESTION 115

When you arrive at an area where a policeman or flagman is directing traffic, you should

A. Maintain your standard speed
B. Slow down and carefully check for other vehicles
C. Maintain your standard speed but be prepared to stop
D. Come to a complete stop and check for other vehicles

Section: Passenger Transport

QUESTION 116

Before you accept cargo or baggage with dangerous materials, you must confirm that the container has which of the following?

A. Hazard label, the material's name, and identification number
B. Hazard label and Material Safety Data Sheet (MSDS)
C. Material's name and identification number
D. Hazard label, country of origin, and material's name

Section: Passenger Transport

QUESTION 117
When you are on the road, you should

A. Scan the road ahead and to the rear
B. Continually scan the road from left to right
C. Remain focused on the road ahead of you
D. Scan the interior of the bus as well as the road ahead, behind and to the sides

Section: Passenger Transport

QUESTION 118

Bus passengers should NOT

A. Stand while on a bus
B. Stand behind the standee line
C. Stand across from other passengers
D. Stand in front of the standee line

Section: Passenger Transport

QUESTION 119

During your pre-trip inspection, which of the following items should you check?

A. Service brakes, parking brake, steering mechanism
B. Horn, windshield wipers, emergency exit handles
C. Fire extinguisher, emergency reflector
D. All of the above

Section: Passenger Transport

QUESTION 120

If you are transporting passengers on a charter bus, you should

A. Allow passengers on the bus 45 minutes prior to departure

B. Not allow passengers on the bus until departure time
C. Insure that the restroom service access panel is open
D. None of the above

Section: Passenger Transport

QUESTION 121

When transporting passengers on charter or intercity buses, you should mention rules regarding safety and comfort

A. Only if a question arises
B. At the first occurrence of a violation
C. Once you are on the road
D. Before the trip is started

Section: Passenger Transport

QUESTION 122

You do not have to stop, but you must slow down and carefully check for other vehicles at

A. Railroad crossings
B. Drawbridges that do not have a traffic light or traffic control attendant
C. Crossings marked as exempt or abandoned
D. None of the above

Section: Passenger Transport

QUESTION 123

Which of the following dangerous material loads is acceptable to transport on a bus?

A. 10 pounds of liquid Class 6 poison
B. 100 pounds of solid Class 6 poison
C. Radioactive materials (less than 2 ounces) in the space occupied by people
D. 10 pounds of Class 1 explosives, other than small arms ammunition

Section: Passenger Transport

QUESTION 124

Which factor(s) should you consider when determining how much liquid to load into a tank?

A. Weight of the liquid
B. Legal weight limits
C. How much the liquid will expand during transit
D. All of the above

Section: Tanker Practice

QUESTION 125

The effects of liquid surge are reduced by

A. Braking far in advance and increasing your stopping distance
B. Starting, stopping and turning smoothly
C. Hauling thicker liquids
D. All of the above

Section: Tanker Practice

QUESTION 126
What should you do to avoid a tanker from rolling over on a curve?

A. Travel at the posted speed limit on a curve
B. Brake aggressively throughout the curve
C. Travel well below the posted speed limit on a curve
D. None of the above

Section: Tanker Practice

QUESTION 127
A baffled tanker has

A. Separate tanks inside the trailer
B. Interior bulkheads with holes that let the liquid flow through
C. A smooth interior, and is frequently used to transport food products
D. Dampers that float on the liquid to slow movement

Section: Tanker Practice

ANSWERS

A1: Correct Answer: C

A2: Correct Answer: A

A3: Correct Answer: A

A4: Correct Answer: A

A5: Correct Answer: B

A6: Correct Answer: B

A7: Correct Answer: E

A8: Correct Answer: C

A9: Correct Answer: E

A10: Correct Answer: C

A11: Correct Answer: A

A12: Correct Answer: B

A13: Correct Answer: B

A14: Correct Answer: E

A15: Correct Answer: B

A16: Correct Answer: B

A17: Correct Answer: D

A18: Correct Answer: A

A19: Correct Answer: C

A20: Correct Answer: B

A21: Correct Answer: B

A22: Correct Answer: B

A23: Correct Answer: B

A24: Correct Answer: B

A25: Correct Answer: B

A26: Correct Answer: B

A27: Correct Answer: B

A28: Correct Answer: B

A29: Correct Answer: B

A30: Correct Answer: D

A31: Correct Answer: D

A32: Correct Answer: D

A33: Correct Answer: B

A34: Correct Answer: B

A35: Correct Answer: B

A36: Correct Answer: A

A37: Correct Answer: B

A38: Correct Answer: E

A39: Correct Answer: F

A40: Correct Answer: C

A41: Correct Answer: A

A42: Correct Answer: C

A43: Correct Answer: D

A44: Correct Answer: E

A45: Correct Answer: A

A46: Correct Answer: A

A47: Correct Answer: A

A48: Correct Answer: D

A49: Correct Answer: A

A50: Correct Answer: A

A51: Correct Answer: D

A52: Correct Answer: D

A53: Correct Answer: B

A54: Correct Answer: C

A55: Correct Answer: C

A56: Correct Answer: C

A57: Correct Answer: D

A58: Correct Answer: C

Explanation

The correct answer is: Compressed air. Air brakes use compressed air for operation and are a safe way to stop large and heavy vehicles if maintained correctly.

A59: Correct Answer: B

A60: Correct Answer: A

A61: Correct Answer: D

A62: Correct Answer: C

Explanation

The correct answer is: Fifth wheel plate. When coupling tractor-semitrailers you need to insure that the fifth wheel plate is greased as required so that friction amid the tractor and trailer does not cause steering difficulties.

A63: Correct Answer: C

Explanation

The correct answer is: Turn the crank in low gear a few extra turns after firm contact with the ground. If you turn the crank in low gear a few extra turns, it will lift some weight off of the tractor which will make it easier for you to unlatch the fifth.

A64: Correct Answer: C

A65: Correct Answer: A

A67: Correct Answer: C

A68: Correct Answer: B

A69: Correct Answer: D

A70: Correct Answer: E

A71: Correct Answer: B

A72: Correct Answer: B

A73: Correct Answer: A

A74: Correct Answer: A

A75: Correct Answer: C

A76: Correct Answer: B

A77: Correct Answer: D

A78: Correct Answer: B

A79: Correct Answer: D

A80: Correct Answer: C

A81: Correct Answer: E

A82: Correct Answer: B

A83: Correct Answer: D

A84: Correct Answer: B

Explanation:

The correct answer is: "Crack-the-whip" effect when making quick lane changes. Rearward amplification is increased in doubles and triples. A conventional double has a rearward amplification of 2.0, which means that it is twice as likely to turn over as a standard 5 axle trailer. A triple has a rearward amplification of 3.5.

A85: Correct Answer: D

Explanation:

The correct answer is: First trailer position (behind the tractor). The lightest trailer should be in the third/last position. Putting the heaviest trailer in the first position behind the trailer will provide the safest handling on the road.

A86: Correct Answer: A

Explanation:

The correct answer is: The dolly tow bar may fly up, possibly causing injury. If you unlock the pintle hook with the dolly still under the rear trailer, it will also be very difficult to re-couple.

A87: Correct Answer: C

Explanation:

The correct answer is: Back first semitrailer in front of dolly tongue. The steps to connect the converter dolly to the front trailer are: back first semitrailer into position in front of dolly tongue; hook dolly to front trailer; lock pintle hook; secure converter gear support in raised position.

A88: Correct Answer: B

Explanation:

The correct answer is: Drive the tractor close to the trailer, connect the emergency line to charge the trailer air tank and disconnect the emergency line. This process will set the trailer emergency brakes (assuming that the slack adjusters are correctly adjusted). You can also chock the wheels as an additional measure.

A89: Correct Answer: B

Explanation

The correct answer is: Supply air to the emergency air line. The trailer air supply control knob is used to control the tractor protection valve. You push the knob in to supply the trailer with air (via the emergency air line) and pull it out to shut off the air and put on the trailer emergency brakes.

A90: Correct Answer: C

Explanation

The correct answer is: Push in the red trailer air supply knob, open the emergency line shut-off valve at the rear of the last trailer and listen for air escaping. To check the service line air flow, you use the trailer hand brake to supply air to the service lines. Go to the rear of the last trailer, open the service line valve and listen for air escaping.

A91: Correct Answer: D

Explanation

The correct answer is: To close the airlines of the last trailer to avoid air from leaking out. Shut- off valves (sometimes referred to as cut-out cocks) are located at the back of trailers used to tow other trailers. These valves allow you to close of the air lines when other trailers are not being towed. Trailer hand valves (also called trolley valves or Johnson bar) work the trailer brakes. The trailer air supply control controls the trailer emergency brakes.

A92: Correct Answer: A

Explanation:

The correct answer is: Fully closed. Shut-off valves (sometimes referred to as cut-out cocks) are located at the back of trailers used to tow other trailers. All valves should be in the open position except on the last trailer which should be in the closed position.

A93: Correct Answer: B

Explanation:

The correct answer is: Fully open. Shut-off valves (sometimes referred to as cut-out cocks) are located at the back of trailers used to tow other trailers. All valves should be in the open position except on the last trailer which should be in the closed position.

A94: Correct Answer: A

A95: Correct Answer: C

Explanation:

The correct answer is: Allow more following distance. Doubles and triples have longer stopping distances and require more following distance. The heaviest semitrailer should go in the first position, not the rear position.

A96: Correct Answer: D

Explanation:

The correct answer is: No space. There should be no space amid the upper and lower fifth wheel after coupling. If there is space, it indicates a difficulties such as the kingpin resting on top of the closed fifth wheel jaws.

A97: Correct Answer: D

A98: Correct Answer: D

Explanation:

The correct answer is: Both service and emergency air lines. Shut-off valves (sometimes referred to as cut-out cocks) are located at the back of trailers used to tow other trailers. They are used for both the service and emergency air lines.

A99: Correct Answer: D

Explanation:

The correct answer is: All of the above. The trailer protection valve's purpose is to keep air in the brake system in case the trailer brakes away or develops a bad leak. If the trailer protection valve malfunctions, then air could be drained away from it.

A100: Correct Answer: B

Explanation:

The correct answer is: Use trolley valve to apply brakes and check to see if you feel the trailer brakes come on. To test the trailer service brakes you should check for standard air pressure, release the parking brakes, and move the vehicle forward slowly.

A101: Correct Answer: C

Explanation:

The correct answer is: Trailer is slightly lower than the center of the fifth wheel. The trailer should be low enough that it is raised slightly when the tractor is backed under it. If the trailer is too low, the trailer nose may become damaged.

A102: Correct Answer: B

Explanation:

The correct answer is: Trailer is slightly lower than the center of the fifth wheel. The trailer should be low enough that it is raised slightly when the tractor is backed under it. If the trailer is too low, the trailer nose may become damaged.

A103 Correct Answer: D

Explanation:

The correct answer is: A and C. When connecting the converter dolly to the rear trailer, the shut-off valves on the last trailer should be CLOSED. The shut-off valves at the rear of the first trailer (and dolly if it is equipped) should be OPEN.

A104: Correct Answer: C

Explanation:

The correct answer is: Close any open access panels (baggage, engine etc.). Your front tires must NOT be recapped or regrouped. Emergency roof hatches may be locked in a partly open position for fresh air, although you should not leave them there are a regular practice.

A105: Correct Answer: C

Explanation:

The correct answer is: Tear gas. Buses must never carry division 2.3 poison gas, liquid class 6 poison, tear gas, or irritating material. Buses may carry small-arms ammunition (labeled ORM-D), emergency hospital supplies, and drugs.

A106: Correct Answer: B

Explanation:
The correct answer is: Small-arms ammunition. Buses may carry small-arms ammunition (labeled ORM-D), emergency hospital supplies, and drugs. Buses should never carry liquid class 6 poisons (such as pesticides). Also, buses should not allow riders to carry on common hazards such as car batteries or gasoline.

A107: Correct Answer: D

Explanation:

The correct answer is: Standee line. Riders are not allowed to stand forward of the rear of the driver's seat. Buses that allow standing must have a "standee line" (two-inch line on the floor behind the driver's seat) to show passengers where they cannot stand.

A108: Correct Answer: C

Explanation:

The correct answer is: Drop the person off at the next scheduled stop or a nearby safe well-lit area. If you have a disruptive passenger, you must ensure their safety as well as the safety of others. You should not discharge the passenger immediately if the area is not a scheduled stop or a safe area.

A109: Correct Answer: B

Explanation:

The correct answer is: Open your forward door to look and listen for approaching train. You should also stop amid 15 and 50 feet before the railroad crossing and never change gears while crossing the tracks.

A110: Correct Answer: C

Explanation:

The correct answer is: Stop at least 50 feet before the draw of the bridge. You are not required to exit your vehicle, but if there is no attendant, you should completely stop your vehicle (not just slow down) and insure that the drawbridge is closed.

A111: Correct Answer: C

Explanation:

The correct answer is: You can use the interlock in place of the parking brake. The interlock is not a substitute for the parking brake - it is intended as an additional safety feature on some urban mass transit coaches.

A112: Correct Answer: B

Explanation:

The correct answer is: Requesting the passengers to leave the bus during refueling. You should evade fueling your bus with passengers on board unless absolutely necessary. You should never refuel in a closed building with passengers on board. Likewise, towing the bus with riders on board, or having conversations with passengers is not suggested.

A113: Correct Answer: C

Explanation:

The correct answer is: Slow down if your bus leans toward the outside of the curve. You should moderate speed for curves even if other drivers don't. The posted speed is safe for cars, but may be too high for buses.

A114: Correct Answer: C

Explanation:

The correct answer is: Before and after your shift. It is significant to inspect your bus before your shift to insure it is safe and to certify that all earlier reported faults have been repaired or addressed. It is also significant to inspect the vehicle.

A115: Correct Answer: B

Explanation:

The correct answer is: Slow down and carefully check for other vehicles. If there is a policeman or flagman directing traffic, you do not have to stop, but you should slow down and carefully check for other vehicles.

A116: Correct Answer: A

Explanation:

The correct answer is: Hazard label, the material's name, and identification number. Most dangerous material cannot be carried on a bus. If the laws allow the transport of the dangerous material, then the shipper is required to mark the container with them.

A117: Correct Answer: D

Explanation:

The correct answer is: Scan the interior of the bus as well as the road ahead, behind and to the sides. When driving it is significant that you focus on both the safety of the bus and of the passengers.
Therefore, you should insure that you scan both them.

A118: Correct Answer: D

Explanation:

The correct answer is: Stand in front of the standee line. The standee line is a two-inch line of the floor (behind the driver's seat) that marks where passengers are allowed to stand. Passengers are NOT allowed to stand in front of the standee line.

A119: Correct Answer: D

Explanation:

The correct answer is: All of the above. During your pre-trip inspection, it is significant to check the vehicle systems (brakes, steering, lights, tires, horn etc.), access doors and panels (emergency exits, baggage and restroom service panels).

A120: Correct Answer: B

Explanation:

The correct answer is: Not allow passengers on the bus until departure time. By not allowing your passengers on the bus until departure time, you lessen the threat of theft or vandalism to the bus.

A121: Correct Answer: D

Explanation:

The correct answer is: Before the trip is started. You should mention comfort and safety rules (i.e., regarding smoking, drinking, use of radios etc.) prior to the start of the trip - this will help you evade difficulties later on.

A122: Correct Answer: C

Explanation:

He correct answer is: Crossings marked as exempt or abandoned. At railroad crossings and drawbridge crossing that do not have a traffic light or traffic control attendant you must stop your bus. You do not have to stop (but must slow down)

A123: Correct Answer: B

Explanation:

The correct answer is: 100 pounds of solid Class 6 poison. Buses must never carry any amount of *liquid* class 6 poison but are allowed to carry up to 100 pounds of *solid* Class 6 poison. Buses should never carry any amount of radioactive material or

A124: Correct Answer: D

Explanation:

The correct answer is: All of the above. Some dense liquids (e.g., some acids) may exceed legal weight limits. Liquids can also expand as they warm. Therefore you should check the weight of the liquid, the legal weight limits, and how much the liquid will expand before determining how much liquid you can safely load.

A125: Correct Answer: D

Explanation:

The correct answer is: All of the above. Liquid surge is caused by the movement of liquid in partially filled tanks. Abrupt start, stops or lane changes will increase the effects of liquid surge. Thicker liquids will tend to move less, which will moderate the effects of liquid surge.

A126: Correct Answer: C

Explanation:

The correct answer is: Travel well below the posted speed limit on a curve. Most rollovers occur around curves. Tests have shown that rollovers can occur at the posted speed limit for a curve, so you should drive well below the posted speed limit. Also, you should slow down before the curve, and then accelerate slightly through the curve. You should not aggressively brake while on the curve.

A127: Correct Answer: B

Explanation:

The correct answer is: Interior bulkheads with holes that let the liquid flow through. Unbaffled tankers have a smooth interior and are frequently referred to as smooth bore tanks.